BRIGHT
IDEA
BOOKS

YOU CAN WORK IN
Dance

by Samantha S. Bell

Raintree is an imprint of Capstone Global Library Limited, a company incorporated in England and Wales having its registered office at 264 Banbury Road, Oxford, OX2 7DY – Registered company number: 6695582

www.raintree.co.uk
myorders@raintree.co.uk

Edited by Charly Haley
Designed by Becky Daum
Production by Claire Vanden Branden
Originated by Capstone Global Library Ltd
Printed and bound in India

ISBN 978 1 4747 7535 9 (hardback)   ISBN 978 1 4747 7359 1 (paperback)
22 21 20 19 18   22 21 20 19 18
10 9 8 7 6 5 4 3 2 1   10 9 8 7 6 5 4 3 2 1

British Library Cataloguing in Publication Data
A full catalogue record for this book is available from the British Library.

Acknowledgements
We would like to thank the following for permission to reproduce photographs: iStockphoto: DragonImages, 8–9, FilippoBacci, 24–25, gradyreese, 30–31, kzenon, 20, Mlenny, 6–7; Shutterstock Images, CREATISTA, 11, criben, 26–27, Diego Cervo, 15, Iakov Filimonov, 19, Igor Bulgarin, 12–13, Jacob Lund, 16–17, Nataliya Hora, 5, T-Design, cover (foreground), Tyler Olson, cover (background), wavebreakmedia, 23, 29. Design Elements: iStockphoto, Red Line Editorial, and Shutterstock Images.

Every effort has been made to contact copyright holders of material reproduced in this book. Any omissions will be rectified in subsequent printings if notice is given to the publisher.

All the internet addresses (URLs) given in this book were valid at the time of going to press. However, due to the dynamic nature of the internet, some addresses may have changed, or sites may have changed or ceased to exist since publication. While the author and publisher regret any inconvenience this may cause readers, no responsibility for any such changes can be accepted by either the author or the publisher.

CONTENTS

CHAPTER 1

PROFESSIONAL
Dancers

The music starts. A dancer comes onto the stage. She moves with the music. The dance may look smooth and easy. But it takes many hours of practice.

A ballet dancer performs set steps.

A hip-hop dancer moves to the beat of the music.

Dancers perform in many different places. You may see them in a play or a movie. They might be on TV or in a music video.

There are many styles of dance. Most dancers are good at one style. Some are **ballet** dancers. Some are **hip-hop** dancers. Some do **tap**, **Latin** or **ballroom** dancing.

NEW MOVES

Some kinds of dance change over time. Hip-hop started in the 1970s. Dancers are still creating new moves.

Dancers practise as a group.

Dancers work very hard. They practise their **routines**.

A dancer must work well with others. Most dancers perform as a group. Some perform with a partner. They spend many hours together.

Most dancers start dancing when they are young. They take lessons from a dance teacher. Later they go to dance school.

CHAPTER 2

CHOREOGRAPHERS

Choreographers create dance routines. They decide the dance steps. Sometimes they choose the music and costumes.

Choreographers use dance to show a story or an idea. They make the movements fit the music. They make something new with each dance.

A choreographer makes sure dancers move in time with each other.

A choreographer creates dances for a musical.

Choreographers may work for dance companies. Dance companies have many dancers. Choreographers may work at schools or dance studios. They might work on **musicals**.

Choreographers must also be good teachers. They lead **rehearsals**. They show the dancers how to do the steps.

Choreographers usually start out as dancers. Some learn by creating dances for friends.

COSTUME DESIGNERS

Costume designers create the dance costumes. They work with choreographers. The costumes must fit the music and movement.

CHAPTER 3

ARTS
Managers

It takes more than just dancers to put on a performance. Someone needs to watch the dance. Arts **managers** bring dancers and audiences together.

Some managers work for dance companies. Others work in theatres. Some manage community projects.

An arts manager watches a dance rehearsal.

Managers work with the business side of dance. They plan events. They handle the money for events. They employ workers. They get people to come to events.

Arts managers must be organized. They should be creative. Good managers love dance.

Some arts managers went to university. Some have dance training.

An arts manager must have good communication skills.

CHAPTER 4

DANCE
Teachers

Dance teachers show pupils how to practise. They teach them how to move safely. They teach them different types of dance.

Teachers decide the dance steps. They teach them to the pupils. The pupils perform the dances.

Some pupils dance for fun. Some want to work as dancers. Dance teachers help them to achieve their goals.

A dance teacher shows young pupils how to move.

A dance teacher may give
private lessons.

Dance teachers must be patient. They must work well with others. They must also be good leaders.

Some teach in a dance studio. Others teach in schools. Some studied dance at university or college.

ON THEIR OWN

Some dance teachers have their own dance studio. They run it as a business.

CHAPTER 5

DANCE Therapists

Dance **therapists** use dance to help others. They work with people of all ages.

Dance therapists want to help people feel good about themselves. They want people to feel **confident**. So they teach people to dance.

A dance therapist helps someone feel better through dance.

A dance therapist uses talking and dance to help someone deal with problems.

Dance therapists help people find ways to **cope** with problems. They help people deal with stress. They help people get along with others.

Some dance therapists work in schools. Others work in **counselling centres**. Some work in hospitals or nursing homes.

Most dance therapists need to get a university degree. They must also know how to dance.

A dancer performs with musicians.

Some dancers perform. Some teach or help others. There are many different ways to work in dance!

GLOSSARY

ballet
style of dance with
set movements

ballroom
style of dance for two people

choreographer
person who makes
dance routines

confident
believing in your abilities

cope
deal with something difficult

counselling centre
place where people can
get professional advice for
personal problems

hip-hop
fast-paced style of dance that
started in African-American
culture

Latin
Latin-American style
of dance such as salsa

manager
person who is in charge of
a project or organization

musical
play on stage with songs and
dancing

rehearsal
time to practise before
a performance

routine
set of movements performed
in a certain order

tap
dance performed in shoes
that make tapping sounds

therapist
person who professionally
helps other people with
their problems

FIND OUT MORE

Want to learn more about different styles of dance? Check out these resources:

Books

Ballroom (Love to Dance), Angela Royston (Raintree, 2014)

Impressive Dance Moves, Ellen Lebrecque (Raintree, 2014)

Mad About Dance, Judith Heneghan (Wayland, 2016)

Street Dance, Rita Storey (Franklin Watts, 2013)

Website

nationalcareersservice.direct.gov.uk/job-profiles/performing-arts-broadcast-and-media

This website tells you about many jobs in dance. Ask an adult or use a dictionary to help you understand any difficult words.

Place to visit

The Victoria and Albert Museum, London

www.vam.ac.uk/page/t/theatre-and-performance-galleries

This museum has an area that focuses on theatre and performance.

ACTIVITY

CREATE YOUR OWN DANCE ROUTINE!

Choose a song. Now create a dance to go with the song. Think about how the words and music make you feel. Create your own dance moves to express those feelings. Perform your dance for family or friends. You can even teach them your new dance routine!

INDEX